JONES & BARTLETT LEARNING INFORMATION SYSTEMS SECURITY & ASSURAN

LABORATORY MANUAL TO ACCOMPANY

Access Control, Authentication, and Public Key Infrastructure

JONES & BARTLETT
LEARNING

World Headquarters
Jones & Bartlett Learning
5 Wall Street
Burlington, MA 01803
978-443-5000
info@jblearning.com
www.jblearning.com

Jones & Bartlett Learning books and products are available through most bookstores and online booksellers. To contact Jones & Bartlett Learning directly, call 800-832-0034, fax 978-443-8000, or visit our website, www.jblearning.com.

This publication is designed to provide accurate and authoritative information in regard to the subject matter covered. It is sold with the understanding that the publisher is not engaged in rendering legal, accounting, or other professional service. If legal advice or other expert assistance is required, the service of a competent professional person should be sought.

Production Credits
Chief Executive Officer: Ty Field
President: James Homer
SVP, Chief Technology Officer: Dean Fossella
SVP, Chief Marketing Officer: Alison M. Pendergast
SVP, Curriculum Solutions: Christopher Will
Author: vLab Solutions, LLC, David Kim, President
Editorial Management: Perspectives, Inc., Phil Graham, President
Reprints and Special Projects Manager: Susan Schultz
Associate Production Editor: Tina Chen
Director of Marketing: Alisha Weisman
Senior Marketing Manager: Andrea DeFronzo
Manufacturing and Inventory Control Supervisor: Amy Bacus
Cover Design: Anne Spencer
Composition: vLab Solutions, LLC
Cover Image: © ErickN/ShutterStock, Inc.
Printing and Binding: Malloy, Inc.
Cover Printing: Malloy, Inc.

ISBN: 978-1-4496-4395-9

6048
Printed in the United States of America
15 14 13   10 9 8 7 6 5 4

Table of Contents

Current Version Date: 07/27/2011

Current Version Date: 07/27/2011

Current Version Date: 07/27/2011

Laboratory #1

Lab #1: Configure Access Controls for User Accounts given a Regulatory Case Study

Learning Objectives and Outcomes

Upon completing this lab, students will be able to complete the following tasks:

- Configure user accounts and access controls in a Windows Server according to a role-based access control design

- Configure user account login credentials and permissions as defined by policy for each user type

- Create and administer Group Policy Objects for the management of Windows Active Directory Domain machines within a common environment

- Apply Group Policy Object definitions and permissions as defined by policy for each user type

- Assign and manage access privileges as per the case study recommendations for proper security controls

Required Setup and Tools

This lab requires that the instructor and student workstations and VMs be connected to the shared, classroom layer 2 switch and physically disconnected from the classroom/building network and public Internet. This will also allow the Instructor to enable the shared, DHCP server to be used for all the VMs used in this equipment-based lab.

NOTE: The instructor will enable the lab's DHCP server by powering on the "DHCPWindows01" server which will allocate a source IP host address to all workstations and VMs enabled. Only 1 DHCP server should be enabled for IP host address allocation on the same IP subnetwork at a given time.

The following equipment is required for this equipment-based lab:

A) Student classroom workstations (with at least 2GB RAM) capable of supporting the removable hard drive with the VM server farm and up to 2 simultaneously running VMs.

NOTE: Only one VM will be running at full speed on a workstation with only 2GB of RAM. If you power-on 2 VMs at once on a workstation with only 2GB of RAM, there will be performance slowdown. For optimal performance, load 2 or more VMs with at least 4GB of RAM in your workstation.

Current Version Date: 07/27/2011

B) Instructor workstations (with at least 4 Gig RAM) that shall act as the Instructor's demo lab workstation. The instructor will display the Instructor VM or other Server Farm VMs on the LCD projector to demo the loading and configuring of the VM Server Farm and execute demonstrations of the hands-on labs using VMware Player.

C) Student workstations will use their own VM Server Farm. VMware Player will be used to run the VMs on both Instructor and Student workstations. It is strongly recommended that the VMs be copied to the local classroom workstation whenever possible to improve performance.

The following summarizes the setup, configuration, and equipment needed to perform Lab #1: "TargetWindows01" is a Windows 2003 Standard Server VM used with VM Server Farm v2. "TargetWindows02" is a newer Windows 2008 Standard Server VM that was released as an upgrade to VM Server Farm v2. "TargetWindows02" VM is now part of the VM Server Farm v3.

Although the "TargetWindows02" 2008 Server is not mandatory to perform this equipment-based lab, it is a more up to date VM to be performing this equipment-based lab.

1. The VM Server Farm (Version 2 or higher) with the following VMs:
   a. A Target Windows 2003 Standard Server VM ("TargetWindows01"); or
   b. A Target Windows 2008 Standard Server VM ("TargetWindows02")

2. A standard classroom workstation must have the following software applications loaded to perform this lab:
   a. VMware Player 3.x
   b. Microsoft Office 2007 or higher for Lab Assessment Questions & Answers

Recommended Procedures

Equipment-Based Lab #1 – Student Steps:

Students should perform the following steps for this equipment-based lab:

1. Connect your removable hard drive to your classroom workstation

---

NOTE: Prior to running the "dcpromo" DNS and Domain Controller configurator, a static IP address MUST be manually assigned to the "TargetWindows0" or "TargetWindows02" VM. This is required for proper DNS and Domain Controller configuration.

Current Version Date: 07/27/2011

Create an Active Directory Domain

2. Power-on only **ONE** of the following Target Windows servers from your VM server farm:

    a. "TargetWindows01" **OR** "TargetWindows02"

3. Target Windows Server Logons and Computer Information is as follows:

    a. Usernames: "administrator", "instructor", or "student" (without quotes)

    b. Password: "ISS316Security" (without quotes, case sensitive)

    c. Target Windows Servers available in the Mock IT Server Farm Version 3:

        i. "TargetWindows01": Windows Server 2003 Standard Edition 32-bit

        ii. "TargetWindows02": Windows Server 2008 Standard Edition 32-bit

    d. Domain Login: These VMs are delivered as stand-alone servers, by running "dcpromo" you will create a new domain, forest, and corresponding users, groups, and permissions

    e. IP Address: Target Windows Servers are configured DHCP by default

4. After you login to the Target Windows Server, verify that your server has a static IP address and is using its own IP as the Primary DNS server by clicking: Start > Control Panel > Network and Sharing. From here, click on your TCP/IP LAN adapter and examine the IP address information

5. If the server does not have a static IP assigned, follow these steps:

    a. Click Start > Control Panel > Network and Sharing the edit your TCP/IP LAN adapter

    b. Configure your network settings as follows:

        ▪ IP Address: 172.30.0.40

        ▪ Subnet Mask: 255.255.255.0

        ▪ Primary DNS Server: 172.30.0.40

NOTE: By using this IP host address in your selected "TargetWindows01" or "TargetWindows02" VM, there will not be any conflicts with other equipment-based labs and VM's used in this course.

---

6. Now create a new Domain Controller for a new Active Directory Forest on the TargetWindows Server by clicking: Start > Run > and typing "**dcpromo**" into the run command prompt box

7. Follow the New Active Directory Domain Wizard to create a new Domain Controller for a new Active Directory Forest

8. Let Windows enable and automatically configure DNS on the new Domain Controller

9. Finalize the new configuration with a reboot of the TargetWindows Server

Domain   1S3230.ProfLillie
NetBios   1S3230 PROF

Current Version Date: 07/27/2011

1S3230 wff 4unow

Create Active Directory Objects and Assign Role-based Access Controls

10. Log into your new Domain Controller as an administrator of the new domain

11. Create the following Global Domain users and groups using the Active Directory Users and Computers management console as follows

12. Click Start -> Administrative Tools -> Active Directory Users and Computers

13. Navigate the tree structure on the left and identify the Users container

> **NOTE:** All Users and Groups are stored in the Users container by default in a new Active Directory domain. Unless there is a specific reason, all users and groups should be created in the default Users container.

14. Right-click the Users container and create the following new Groups:

    a. InspectorGeneral

    b. FAR

    c. SenateChairs

    d. AwardedContracts

15. Right-click the Users container and create the following new Users with the corresponding group membership:

    a. 'MBH1234' user account (use 'MBH!234pass' for the password) – member of InspectorGeneral group

    b. 'RJX-123' user account (use 'RJX-!23pass' for the password) – member of InspectorGeneral and AwardedContracts groups

    c. 'RXJ0123' user account (use 'RXJ0!23pass' for the password) – member of AwardedContracts group

    d. 'MBR0011' user account (use 'MBR00!!pass' for the password) – member of SenateChairs group

    e. The "Everyone" Group should be added as a member of the FAR group

16. Create four new folders as follows:

    a. C:\FAR – This folder will contain miscellaneous shared files for the Federal Acquisition Regulation

    b. C:\FAR\SCfiles – Folder for shared Senate Chairs (SC) user files

    c. C:\FAR\IGfiles – Folder for shared Inspector General (IG) user files

    d. C:\FAR\ACfiles – Folder for shared Awarded Contracts (AC) user files

Current Version Date: 07/27/2011

17. Determine what type of access controls are needed to allow the following actions by the groups defined in the following sections:

    a. Allow Inspector General users to read and write files in C:\ FAR\IGfiles

    b. Allow Senate Chairs users to read and write files in C:\ FAR\SCfiles

    c. Allow Awarded Contracts users to read and write files in C:\ FAR\ACfiles and C:\ FAR\SCfiles

Create Group Policy Objects Definitions

18. Launch Active Directory Users and Computers on the TargetWindows Server

19. Click Start -> Administrative Tools -> Active Directory Users and Computers

20. In the tree view, expand Forest -> Domains -> "yournewdomain" -> then right click the "domain name" and click Properties

21. Select 'Group Policy Objects' and click 'New"

22. Create five new Group Policy Objects and name them as follows:

    a. Inspector General

    b. Federal Acquisition Regulation (FAR)

    c. Awarded Contracts

    d. Senate Chairs

    e. Password GPO

23. Open the context menu (right click) of the newly created Password GPO and select 'Edit…'

24. In the Group Policy Management Editor, expand Computer Configuration -> Policies -> Windows Settings -> Security Settings -> Account policies

25. Select 'Password Policy'.

26. Double-click 'Password must meet complexity requirements' and click "Enable"

27. Click 'OK'

28. Double-click 'Minimum Password Length' and enter 8. Click 'OK'

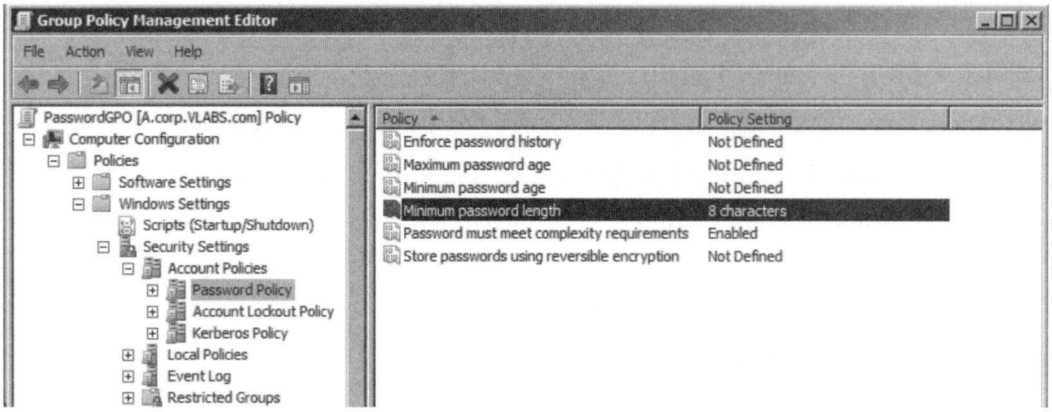

Figure 1 –Microsoft Windows Group Policy Management Editor

29. Close the Group Policy Management Editor

30. Open the context menu for the domain in Active Directory Users and Computers then select 'Link an Existing GPO…"

31. Select 'PasswordGPO' and click 'OK'

32. Explain to the students how to "Link" each of the four other newly created GPOs to the corresponding Objects in Active Directory as defined in the following table:

Group Policy Object	Files Created	User Assigned
Inspector General	Annual audit	MBH1234 RJX-123 FAR
	Closed Investigations	Everyone
	No Action Required	Everyone
Federal Acquisition Regulation (FAR)	None	Everyone
Awarded Contracts	None	RXJ0123
Senate Chairs	Limited life	Senate Chairs MBR0011

Figure 2 – User Access Control Requirements

Current Version Date: 07/27/2011

Deliverables

Upon completion of Lab #1: Assess the Impact on Access Controls for a Regulatory Case Study; students are required to provide the following deliverables:

1. Lab #1 – Group Policy Object Access /Control Requirements
2. Lab #1 – Lab Assessment Questions & Answers

Evaluation Criteria and Rubrics

The following are the evaluation criteria and rubrics for Lab #1 that the students must perform:

1. Was the student able to configure user accounts and access controls in a Windows Server according to a role-based access control design? – [**20%**]

2. Was the student able to configure user account login credentials and permissions as defined by policy for each user type? - [**20%**]

3. Was the student able to create and administer Group Policy Objects for the management of Windows Active Directory Domain machines within a common environment? – [**20%**]

4. Was the student able to apply Group Policy Object definitions and permissions as defined by policy for each user type? – [**20%**]

5. Was the student able to assign and manage access privileges as per the case study recommendations for proper security controls? – [**20%**]

Current Version Date: 07/27/2011

Lab #1 – Group Policy Object Assessment Worksheet

Course Name & Number: _____

Student Name: _____

Instructor Name: _____

Lab Due Date: _____

Overview

For this lab, the students must first define a Group Policy Object and the user access control requirements matrix. As part of this lab's deliverables, the students must submit screen captures of the user account configurations, user accounts associated with Group Policy objects, and permissions assigned to each user account.

Group Policy Object	Files Created	User Assigned

Current Version Date: 07/27/2011

Lab #1 – Assessment Worksheet

Assess the Impact on Access Controls for a Regulatory Case Study

Course Name & Number: _____

Student Name: _____

Instructor Name: _____

Lab Due Date: _____

Overview

The students will create an Active Directory domain as well as user and group objects within the new domain. He/she will then create directories and assign permissions based on the required access control as defined in the matrix below. Group Policy Objects will also be created and linked to Objects within the domain to enforce security settings.

Lab Assessment Questions & Answers

1. What does DACL stands for and what does it mean?

2. Why would you add permissions to a group instead of the individual? What policy definition do you think is required to support this type of access control implementation?

Current Version Date: 07/27/2011

3. List the 5 different access control permissions that can be enabled on user folders and data within a Microsoft Windows Server.

4. What is the lowest level of permission you can enable for a user who must view the contents of a folder and its files? Why is this type of permission necessary?

5. What are other available Password Policy options that could be enforced within a Microsoft Windows Server to improve security?

6. Is using the option to 'Store passwords using reversible encryption' a good security practice? Why or why not? When should you enable the option to 'Store passwords using reversible encryption'?

Current Version Date: 07/27/2011

7. What's the difference between a Local Group Policy and a Domain Group Policy?

8. In what order are all available Group Policies applied?

9. What is an Administrative Template as it refers to Windows Group Policy Objects?

10. What is the GPMC? How can GPMC help ensure proper access controls are implemented correctly?

Current Version Date: 07/27/2011

Laboratory #2

Lab #2: Design Infrastructure Access Controls for an IT Infrastructure

Learning Objectives and Outcomes

Upon completing this lab, students will be able to complete the following tasks:

- Assess the impact of unauthorized access throughout the seven domains of a typical IT infrastructure for an organization

- Identify where security controls are needed within the seven domains of a typical IT infrastructure to ensure confidentiality, integrity, and availability (C-I-A) of information and system access

- Specify what security access controls can mitigate the risk from unauthorized access throughout the seven domains of a typical IT infrastructure

- Apply the physical and logical access control solutions to assist with an overall layered security strategy throughout the seven domains of a typical IT infrastructure

- Define the requirements for an access control policy definition that encompasses proper security controls throughout the seven domains of a typical IT infrastructure

Required Setup and Tools

This is a paper-based lab.

The standard lab computer with Microsoft Office 2007 or higher is required for this lab. Students will need to review the seven domains of a typical IT infrastructure diagram (Figure 3), work together in groups, and answer the Lab #2 – Assessment Worksheet and Lab #2 – Assessment Questions using Microsoft Word.

Recommended Procedures

Lab #2 – Student Steps:

Students should perform the following steps:

1. Review the seven domains of a typical IT infrastructure:
   a. User Domain
   b. Workstation Domain
   c. Local Area Network (LAN) Domain
   d. Local Area Network (LAN) – to – Wide Area Network (WAN) Domain

  e. Wide Area Network (WAN) Domain

  f. Remote Access Domain

  g. Systems/Application Domain

  h. Participate in classroom discussions about regarding the following questions:

- What if there were no access controls throughout the seven domains of a typical IT infrastructure?

- What would an attacker be able to do?

- Why is a layered access control solution required for a typical IT infrastructure?

- How does having layers of access controls help mitigate the risk exposure from unauthorized access?

2. Give examples of the access control security countermeasures throughout the seven domains of an IT infrastructure:

  a. User Domain

    i. Authentication Controls

    ii. Security Employee Training and Awareness (SETA)

    iii. Employee/Contractor background checks....

  b. Workstation Domain

    i. Host-based internal firewalls

    ii. Anti-virus software and monitoring

    iii. Patch management, etc...

  c. Local Area Network (LAN) Domain

    i. Firewalls

    ii. Backup/Restore

    iii. Monitoring, etc...

  d. Local Area Network (LAN) to Wide Area Network (WAN) Domain

    i. IDS/IPS

    ii. DMZ

    iii. Firewalls

    iv. Traffic Monitoring

    v. ACLs, etc...

  e. Wide Area Network (WAN) Domain

    i. Firewalls

    ii. Traffic Monitoring

Current Version Date: 07/27/2011

        iii. Content Monitoring, etc…

   f. Remote Access Domain

        i. Encryption, etc…

        ii. IPSEC

        iii. VPN through Internet

        iv. SSL through Internet

        v. Multi-factor Authentication

   g. Systems/Application Domain

        i. Role-based access controls

        ii. Stringent file system and data access and permissions

        iii. Multi-factor authentication

        iv. Data and hard drive encryption

3. Discuss how these security controls and security countermeasures help achieve confidentiality, integrity and availability of information systems and data

4. Discuss how a layered access control strategy helps mitigate risk throughout the seven domains of a typical IT infrastructure

5. Complete the access controls design worksheet matrix for each of the seven domains of a typical IT infrastructure

Deliverables

Upon completion of Lab #2 - Design Infrastructure Access Controls for an IT Infrastructure, students are required to provide the following deliverables:

1. Lab #2 – Access Controls Design Worksheet Matrix
2. Lab #2 – Lab Assessment Questions & Answers

Evaluation Criteria and Rubrics

The following are the evaluation criteria and rubrics for Lab #2 that the students must perform:

1. Was the student able to identify where security controls are needed within the seven domains of a typical IT infrastructure to ensure confidentiality, integrity, and availability (C-I-A) of information and system access? – **[20%]**

2. Was the student able to specify what security access controls can mitigate the risk from unauthorized access throughout the seven domains of a typical IT infrastructure? – **[20%]**

Current Version Date: 07/27/2011

3. Was the student able to relate the impact of unauthorized access throughout the seven domains of a typical IT infrastructure for an organization? – [20%]

4. Was the student able to apply physical and logical access control solutions to assist with an overall layered security strategy throughout the seven domains of a typical IT infrastructure? – [20%]

5. Was the student able to define the requirements for an access control policy that encompasses proper security controls throughout the seven domains of a typical IT infrastructure? – [20%]

Current Version Date: 07/27/2011

Lab #2 – IT Domain Controls Assessment Worksheet
Design Infrastructure Access Controls for a Network Diagram

Course Name & Number: _____

Student Name: _____

Instructor Name: _____

Lab Due Date: _____

Overview

Fill in the following matrix with security controls and security countermeasures to implement sound access controls throughout the seven domains of a typical IT infrastructure. Specify whether the security control or security countermeasure achieves C-I-A and how it enhances security for that domain.

IT Domain	Controls to Implement within Domains	IT Asset or Entity Requiring Security Controls	Are Confidentiality, Integrity, and Availability Achieved?

IT Domain	Controls to Implement within Domains	IT Asset or Entity Requiring Security Controls	Are Confidentiality, Integrity, and Availability Achieved?

Current Version Date: 07/27/2011

IT Domain	Controls to Implement within Domains	IT Asset or Entity Requiring Security Controls	Are Confidentiality, Integrity, and Availability Achieved?

Current Version Date: 07/27/2011

IT Domain	Controls to Implement within Domains	IT Asset or Entity Requiring Security Controls	Are Confidentiality, Integrity, and Availability Achieved?

Current Version Date: 07/27/2011

IT Domain	Controls to Implement within Domains	IT Asset or Entity Requiring Security Controls	Are Confidentiality, Integrity, and Availability Achieved?

Current Version Date: 07/27/2011

IT Domain	Controls to Implement within Domains	IT Asset or Entity Requiring Security Controls	Are Confidentiality, Integrity, and Availability Achieved?

Current Version Date: 07/27/2011

IT Domain	Controls to Implement within Domains	IT Asset or Entity Requiring Security Controls	Are Confidentiality, Integrity, and Availability Achieved?

Current Version Date: 07/27/2011

IT Domain	Controls to Implement within Domains	IT Asset or Entity Requiring Security Controls	Are Confidentiality, Integrity, and Availability Achieved?

Current Version Date: 07/27/2011

Lab #2 – Assessment Worksheet

Design Infrastructure Access Controls for a Network Diagram

Course Name & Number: _____

Student Name: _____

Instructor Name: _____

Lab Due Date: _____

Overview

In this lab students will review and discuss risk exposure due to unauthorized access through the seven domains of a typical IT infrastructure. Specific security controls and security countermeasures will be identified throughout the seven domains of a typical IT infrastructure providing students with a layered security approach. Students will be able to answer the following questions upon completing this lab:

- What if there were no access controls throughout the seven domains of a typical IT infrastructure?
- What would an attacker be able to do?
- Why is a layered access control solution required for a typical IT infrastructure?
- How does having layers of access controls help mitigate the risk exposure from unauthorized access?

Lab Assessment Questions & Answers

1. Why is it important to perform a risk assessment on the systems, applications, and data prior to designing layered access controls?

Current Version Date: 07/27/2011

2. What purpose does a Data Classification Standard have on designing layered access control systems?

3. You are tasked with creating a Microsoft Windows Enterprise Patch Management solution for an organization, but you have no budget. What options does Microsoft provide?

4. How does network monitoring, performance monitoring, alarming, and incident response help secure the IT infrastructure?

5. Provide an example of multi-factor authentication and identify an application that you think would require multi-factor authentication.

6. In which of the seven domains of a typical IT infrastructure would be policy definitions for implementation of anti-virus application/tool as a security countermeasure? Explain.

Current Version Date: 07/27/2011

7. What is the difference between a Host-based Firewall and a Network-based Firewall? What domains of the typical IT infrastructure would you deploy each of these within? Explain how firewalls help mitigate risk exposure by preventing or blocking unauthorized access.

8. Give at least 3 examples of controls typically implemented in the User Domain. Explain these controls.

9. Provide 3 examples of encrypted remote access communications commonly used through the public Internet (i.e., remote access via Internet).

10. Which domain within a typical IT infrastructure is the weakest link? From an access control perspective, why is the User Domain the greatest risk?

11. True or False. It is a best practice to enable both a host-based IP stateful firewall in servers and workstation along with a perimeter, network-based IP stateful firewall for a layered security solution.

12. What types of physical access controls can be implemented to authenticate a physical human prior to allowing entrance into a data center or telecommunications wiring closet?

13. Which of the seven domains of a typical IT infrastructure represents the greatest risk or threat from the outside world and attackers?

14. True or False. It is a best practice to enable an organization-wide Access Control Policy Definition that encompasses all seven domains of a typical IT infrastructure and is properly aligned to a Data Classification Standard.

15. True or False. Organizations that implement an Acceptable Use Policy (AUP) can address access controls within this policy definition.

Current Version Date: 07/27/2011

Laboratory #3

Lab #3: Identify & Classify Data for Access Control Requirements

Learning Objectives and Outcomes

Upon completing this lab, students will be able to complete the following tasks:

- Assess the impact unauthorized access and security breaches have on both private sector and public sector organizations

- Define an organization-wide access control policy for all types of data used throughout the IT infrastructure

- Align an organizational access control policy to accommodate the requirements of a data classification standard

- Develop a plan to classify data and implement proper security controls based on the data classification to ensure privacy and confidentiality of privacy data

- Define an access control policy framework that defines the proper implementation for access throughout the seven domains of a typical IT infrastructure

Required Setup and Tools

This lab requires that the instructor and student workstations and VMs be connected to the shared, classroom layer 2 switch and physically disconnected from the classroom/building network and public Internet. This will also allow the Instructor to enable the shared, DHCP server to be used for all the VMs used in this equipment-based lab.

NOTE: The instructor will enable the lab's DHCP server by powering on the "DHCPWindows01" server which will allocate a source IP host address to all workstations and VMs enabled. Only 1 DHCP server should be enabled for IP host address allocation on the same IP subnetwork at a given time.

The following equipment is required for this equipment-based lab:

A) Student classroom workstations (with at least 2GB RAM) capable of supporting the removable hard drive with the VM server farm and up to 2 simultaneously running VMs.

Current Version Date: 07/27/2011

NOTE: Only one VM will be running at full speed on a workstation with only 2GB of RAM. If you power-on 2 VMs at once on a workstation with only 2GB of RAM, there will be performance slowdown. For optimal performance, load 2 or more VMs with at least 4GB of RAM in your workstation.

B) Instructor workstations (with at least 4 Gig RAM) that shall act as the Instructor's demo lab workstation. The instructor will display the Instructor VM or other Server Farm VMs on the LCD projector to demo the loading and configuring of the Mock IT Server Farm and execute demonstrations of the equipment-based labs using VMware Player.

C) Student workstations will use their own Mock IT Server Farm. VMware Player will be used to run the VMs on both Instructor and Student workstations. It is strongly recommended that the VMs be copied to the local classroom workstation whenever possible to improve performance.

The following summarizes the setup, configuration, and equipment needed to perform Lab #3:
"TargetWindows01" is a Windows 2003 Standard Server VM used with VM Server Farm v2.
"TargetWindows02" is a newer Windows 2008 Standard Server VM that was released as an upgrade to VM Server Farm v2. "TargetWindows02" VM is now part of the VM Server Farm v3.

Although the "TargetWindows02" 2008 Server is not mandatory to perform this equipment-based lab, it is a more up to date VM to be performing this equipment-based lab.

1. The VM Server Farm (Version 2 or higher) with the following VMs:
   a. A Target Windows 2003 Standard Server VM ("TargetWindows01"); or
   b. A Target Windows 2008 Standard Server VM ("TargetWindows02")

2. A standard classroom workstation must have the following software applications loaded to perform this lab:
   a. VMware Player 3.x
   b. Microsoft Office 2007 or higher for Lab Assessment Questions & Answers

Recommended Procedures

Equipment-Based Lab #3 – Student Steps:

Students should perform the following steps for this equipment-based lab:

1. Connect your removable hard drive to your classroom workstation

Current Version Date: 07/27/2011

NOTE: If your workstation has only 2GB of RAM, then only two VMs can be powered-on at once for optimal performance. For this lab, you can load both the "Student" VM and the "TargetWindows01" VM - Windows 2003 Server or the "TargetWindows02" VM – Windows 2008 Server.

2. Review the Data Classification Standard provided in Table 1

Table 1: Data Classification Standard

Data Classification Scheme		
Classification	**Potential Impact**	**Example Data Types**
Public	➢ None or limited ➢ mention in local media; ➢ no impact on operations, financial performance or public image	Published documents, web pages, newspaper advertisements, non-sensitive, information
Internal Use Only	Limited impact from negative publicity, ➢ slight image or financial harm not prolonged or severe in nature	Internal memorandums of operations, continuing contracts, private customer information, short-term operating results and strategy
Confidential	More severe that Limited ➢ impact from negative publicity up to 6 months ➢ moderate image or financial harm < $5 million over 6 – 12 months	Critical and sensitive operating reports, personnel records, pay records, medical records, severe workforce management information, Periodic financial information reported to the public
Restricted	Severe impairment to public image and financial operations ➢ Impairs customer and public trust ➢ >$10 million loss in 3 months ➢ Sustained negative publicity expected for 1 or more years ➢ Impairs ability to execute operation and strategic 3 – 5 years in development and execution.	Strategic plans, communications with the board of directors or with Joint Venture boards of directors, Internal investigations, strategic expansion plans and associated workforce management

3. Review the Job Roles and Access Controls / Network Connectivity Requirements in Table 2

Current Version Date: 07/27/2011

Table 2: Job Roles and Network Connectivity mode

Acme Incorporated	
Individual Organization Roles	Network Connectivity
➢ CEO – Chief Executive Officer	Workstation, mobile pc and iPhone
➢ Remote Plant Manager	Workstation via remote access
➢ SW Area General Mgr	Workstation – network connected
➢ SVP International Acquisitions	mobile pc and iPhone
➢ Executive VP_HR	Workstation, mobile pc and iPhone
➢ EVP Marketing	Workstation, mobile pc and iPhone
➢ SW Store Manager	Workstation
➢ NWR Store Sales Clerk	Cash register - network access for downloads
➢ NWR Receiving Clerk	RF for inventory management
➢ Public Customer	Internet only
➢ Online Customer	Internet
➢ Corporate Controller	Workstation, mobile pc and iPhone
➢ Information Security Specialist	Workstation, mobile pc and iPhone

4. Boot up and log into the "TargetWindows01" server using the following credentials:

   Login ID: "student"

   Password: "ISS316Security" (case sensitive)   *GROUP POLICY OBJECTS*

5. Create Users, Groups and GPOs as defined in Table 1 and Table 2 above

6. Manage properties/security of the groups and add users accounts

Deliverables

Upon completion of Lab #3: Identify & Classify Data for Access Control Requirements, students are required to provide the following deliverables:

1. Lab #3 – Data Classification Standard Assessment Worksheet

2. Lab #3 – Assessment Questions & Answers

Current Version Date: 07/27/2011

Evaluation Criteria and Rubrics

The following are the evaluation criteria and rubrics for Lab #3 that the students must perform:

- Was the student able to assess the impact unauthorized access and security breaches have on both private sector and public sector organizations? – **[20%]**

- Was the student able to define an organization-wide access control policy for all types of data used throughout the IT infrastructure? – **[20%]**

- Was the student able to align an organizational access control policy to accommodate the requirements of a data classification standard? – **[20%]**

- Was the student able to develop a plan to classify data and implement proper security controls based on the data classification to ensure privacy and confidentiality of privacy data? – **[20%]**

- Was the student able to define an access control policy framework that defines the proper implementation for access throughout the seven domains of a typical IT infrastructure? – **[20%]**

Current Version Date: 07/27/2011

Lab #3 – Data Classification Matrix Assessment Worksheet

Course Name & Number: _____

Student Name: _____

Instructor Name: _____

Lab Due Date: _____

Overview

In this lab, the student will review and fill out the Data Classification Standard Matrix based on the information provided in Table 1 and Table 2 of this lab. In the Data Classification Standard Matrix, classify the data by inserting an "X" in the column. Each data item can have only classification. Then align the appropriate job roles (i.e., roles-based access controls) that should have access to the data based on the job function listed.

Data Classification Standard Matrix

Acme Incorporated					
Data/Information Classification Matrix					
Document to Classify	**Public**	**Internal Use Only**	**Confidential**	**Restricted**	**Who Should Have Access**
Monthly Terminations and new hire report					
Contract for long term lease of in Singapore					

Current Version Date: 07/27/2011

Acme Incorporated					
Data/Information Classification Matrix					
Document to Classify	**Public**	**Internal Use Only**	**Confidential**	**Restricted**	**Who Should Have Access**
NWR receiving report					
China sales forecast with projected revenue based on 3 year expansion plan					
NWR Sales results by product category					
Community involvement information published on Corporate Intranet released by Public Affairs					
NWR manpower workforce reduction					
SW Weekly store operating results					

Current Version Date: 07/27/2011

Acme Incorporated					
Data/Information Classification Matrix					
Document to Classify	**Public**	**Internal Use Only**	**Confidential**	**Restricted**	**Who Should Have Access**
Strategic planning documents for changing core organizational functions					
Online product catalog					
Executive reports to the Board of Directors					
Internal fraud investigation from SW region involving the SW Area General Manager					
Report of a minor <$50 credit card fraud perpetrated by a customer at a Eastern store					

Current Version Date: 07/27/2011

Lab #3 – Assessment Worksheet

Identify & Classify Data for Access Control Requirements

Course Name & Number: _____

Student Name: _____

Instructor Name: _____

Lab Due Date: _____

Overview

This lab provides the student with the opportunity to develop a data classification standard with procedures and guidelines to classify data access based on the job responsibilities – not an organizational position. In this lab, students aligned a data classification standard with the job function and roles that are required to access specific data. This alignment allows access controls policy definition to be properly implemented throughout the IT infrastructure to mitigate risk from unauthorized access.

Lab Assessment Questions & Answers

1. What is the Data Classification Standard used in the U.S. Department of Defense (DoD)/Military? Google "Data Classification Standard + DoD". Summarize the different data classifications.

2. Describe one way to help prevent unauthorized users from logging onto another person's user account and accessing his/her data.

Current Version Date: 07/27/2011

3. What permissions are necessary to allow an Active Directory Group called AD_Group to read and write files in a sensitive directory such as C:\ERPdocuments\HRfiles?

4. How would you apply the permissions (ACLs) stated above (M,RX) to the AD_Group on C:\ERPdocuments\HRfiles *from the command prompt* using built-in Windows tools?

5. When adding permissions to a directory in an Active Directory Domain, would you prefer to add Groups or individual User accounts to said directories? Explain.

6. Based on Microsoft's Step-by-Step Guide on Understanding GPOs http://technet.microsoft.com/en-us/library/bb742376.aspx what is the significance of the "Block Inheritance" feature of GPOs and why would it be used?

7. What is the importance of the Security Groups created and why would we setup Security Group Filtering for GPOs as we have done?

Current Version Date: 07/27/2011

8. Explain the Principle of Least Privilege.

9. How does a Data Classification Standard influence your access control strategy?

10. List and explain at least 1 benefit derived from properly implementing the Principle of Least Privilege.

Current Version Date: 07/27/2011

Laboratory #4

Lab #4: Implement Organizational Wide LAN and WLAN Access Controls within the LAN Domain

Learning Objectives and Outcomes

Upon completing this lab, students will be able to complete the following tasks:

1. Review a case study on the access control policies and data classification standard for an organization

2. Assess the impact that unauthorized access to a LAN or WLAN has on both private sector and public sector organizations

3. Configure the internal firewall for a Microsoft Windows Server and Windows XP Workstation based on a policy definition

4. Draft a WLAN security implementation plan to address confidentiality, integrity, and availability of WLAN services

5. Develop an implementation plan regarding the proper deployment of organization-wide access controls throughout the seven domains of a typical IT infrastructure

Required Setup and Tools

This lab requires that the instructor and student workstations and VMs be connected to the shared, classroom layer 2 switch and physically disconnected from the classroom/building network and public Internet. This will also allow the Instructor to enable the shared, DHCP server to be used for all the VMs used in this equipment-based lab.

NOTE: The instructor will enable the lab's DHCP server by powering on the "DHCPWindows01" server which will allocate a source IP host address to all workstations and VMs enabled. Only 1 DHCP server should be enabled for IP host address allocation on the same IP subnetwork at a given time.

The following equipment is required for this equipment-based lab:

A) Student classroom workstations (with at least 2GB RAM) capable of supporting the removable hard drive with the VM server farm and up to 2 simultaneously running VMs.

Current Version Date: 07/27/2011

NOTE: Only one VM will be running at full speed on a workstation with only 2GB of RAM. If you power-on 2 VMs at once on a workstation with only 2GB of RAM, there will be performance slowdown.

B) Instructor workstations (with at least 4 Gig RAM) that shall act as the Instructor's demo lab workstation. The instructor will display the Instructor VM or other Server Farm VMs on the LCD projector to demo the loading and configuring of the VM Server Farm and execute demonstrations of the equipment-based labs using VMware Player.

C) Student workstations will use their own VM Server Farm. VMware Player will be used to run the VMs on both Instructor and Student workstations. It is strongly recommended that the VMs be copied to the local classroom workstation whenever possible to improve performance.

The following summarizes the setup, configuration, and equipment needed to perform Lab #4:
"TargetWindows01" is a Windows 2003 Standard Server VM used with VM Server Farm v2.
"TargetWindows02" is a newer Windows 2008 Standard Server VM that was released as an upgrade to
VM Server Farm v2. "TargetWindows02" VM is now part of the VM Server Farm v3.

Although the "TargetWindows02" Windows 2008 server VM is not mandatory to perform this
equipment-based lab, it is a more up to date VM to be performing this equipment-based lab.

Recommended Procedures

Equipment-Based Lab #4 – Student Steps:

Students should perform the following steps for this equipment-based lab:

1. Connect your removable hard drive to your classroom workstation

2. Power-up and log into the "Student" and "TargetWindows01" VM (or "TargetWindow02")
   Login ID: "student"
   Password: "ISS316Security" (case sensitive)

3. Enable your DOS command prompt (Start-> Run-> 'cmd') and type "ipconfig" from the command prompt and then "ping" your allocated IP host address 172.30.0.__ , and the DHCP server 172.30.0.10.

Current Version Date: 07/27/2011

NOTE: If the workstations in your physical classroom have only 2GB of RAM then only two VMs can be powered-on at once. For this lab, you can load both the Instructor VM and the "TargetWindows01" Windows 2003 Server or "TargetWindows02"- Windows 2008 Server. The DHCP server must be enabled on a different workstation that is connected to the classroom layer 2 switches.

4. Perform a demonstration of a successful PING and FTP file transfer FROM the "Student" VM TO "TargetWindows01" to demonstrate the default settings of a Windows internal firewall if enabled

Implement the Default Microsoft Windows Internal Firewall

5. Configure the host-based firewall on "TargetWindows01" AND the "Student" VM based on the following organizational policy as follows :

    *   Start -> Control Panel -> Select 'Windows Firewall'

6. Add Yahoo! Messenger to Windows Firewall's exception list

    *   If the ICS service isn't turned on you will get a message box asking you to turn it on. Select 'yes' to turn on ICS

7. Turn Windows Firewall On by clicking the 'On' check mark under 'General'

    a. Leave "Don't allow exceptions" unchecked

    b. Click the 'Ok' button to accept changes

    c. Go back into Windows Firewall

8. Select the "Exceptions" tab at the top of the window

    a. Click the 'Add Program' button under Programs and Services

    b. Select Yahoo! Messenger IM Chat under the programs list

    c. If Yahoo! Messenger is not listed, you will have to specify the programs location by clicking the 'Browse' button and selecting the programs location.

9. Block the following applications:

    -   TELNET
    -   TFTP
    -   SNMP
    -   ICMP echo-request
    -   ICMP echo-reply

10. Allow the following applications under ADVANCED settings:

    -   FTP

Current Version Date: 07/27/2011

- SMTP
- POP3
- HTTPS
- HTTP

11. Click the 'Advanced' Tab under the Windows Firewall window

12. Click the 'Settings' button under 'Network Connection Settings'

13. Select the following services by clicking the checkmark next to their names:
    - FTP
    - SMTP
    - POP3
    - HTTPS
    - HTTP

14. All other services will be blocked; the following services should not have a checkmark:
    - TELNET
    - TFTP
    - SNMP

15. Select the 'ICMP' tab at the top of the plane next to services

16. Uncheck every selection in the list (This will block all ICMP echo-reply and ICMP echo-request)

17. Open Windows Security Center from the Control Panel of the "TargetWindows01" server

    a. Start -> Control Panel -> Windows Security

19. Click and run Windows Firewall and demo the settings and configuration parameters listed under GENERAL, EXCEPTIONS, and ADVANCED

20. Display the DEFAULT settings for Windows Firewall

21. Demo how to enable exception rules and advanced settings such as port number filtering

22. Perform a validation test to verify that the exception rules and advanced settings work properly by attempting the following applications from the "Instructor" VM to the "TargetWindows01" VM:

    a. Test and verify PING does not work (from the DOS> prompt)

    b. Test and verify TFTP does not work (use TFTPd32 client & server)

    c. Test and verify FTP does work (use FileZilla client & server)

NOTE: The Instructor will provide you with the following PDF document from the U.S. Department of Defense (DoD) regarding WLAN security.

http://iase.disa.mil/stigs/downloads/zip/unclassified_wireless_stig_v6r2_20100423.zip

---

Current Version Date: 07/27/2011

WLAN Research Portion

23. Extract the zip file then open and review the U_Wireless_STIG_ V6R2_Final_20100423.pdf
    document (WinZip evaluation copy can be downloaded from the Internet if needed here:
    www.winzip.com)

24. Discuss section on "How to Perform a Wireless Review"

    a.   Sample Interview Questions

    b.   Wireless Process Matrix

25. Discuss WLAN compliance requirements

26. Discuss WLAN network devices

27. Discuss WLAN clients

28. PDAs, Cell-phones and Non-wireless e-mail device compliance requirements

Deliverables

Upon completion of Lab #4: Implement Organizational Wide LAN and WLAN Access Controls within
the LAN Domain, students are required to provide the following deliverables:

1.   Lab #4 – ACL and WLAN Assessment Worksheet: Use the tables to correctly and effectively
     respond to the wireless and network security questions. With the completed table submit screen
     image prints/captures to show configuration is effective and implemented.

2.   Lab #4 – Assessment Worksheet with answers to the assessment questions

Evaluation Criteria and Rubrics

The following are the evaluation criteria and rubrics for Lab #4 that the students must perform:

1.   Was the student able to review a case study on the access control policies and data classification
     standard for an organization? – **[20%]**

2.   Was the student able to assess the impact that unauthorized access to a LAN or WLAN has on
     both private sector and public sector organizations – **[20%]**

3.   Was the student able to configure the internal firewall for a Microsoft Windows Server and
     Windows XP Workstation based on a policy definition? – **[20%]**

4.   Was the student able to draft a WLAN security implementation plan to address confidentiality,
     integrity, and availability of WLAN services? – **[20%]**

5.   Was the student able to develop an implementation plan regarding the proper deployment of
     organization-wide access controls throughout the seven domains of a typical IT infrastructure? –
     [20%]

Current Version Date: 07/27/2011

Lab #4 – ACL and Windows Firewall Assessment Worksheet

Course Name & Number: _____

Student Name: _____

Instructor Name: _____

Lab Due Date: _____

Overview

Review the default settings for your Windows Server / Workstation internal host-based firewall and indicate what you would recommend.

Access Control Lists (ACLs) and Firewall Design Worksheet:

GENERAL

_____ – Recommended (Firewall On/Off)

_____ – Don't Allow Exception Rules (On/Off)

_____ – Not Recommended (On/Off)

EXCEPTIONS

_____ – File Print Sharing

_____ – Remote Assistance

_____ – Remote Desktop

_____ – uPnP Framework

ADVANCED

_____ – Network Connection Settings

    _____ – 1394 Connections

    _____ – Cisco AnyConnect VPN

    _____ – Local Area Connection

    _____ – Wireless Network Connection

_____ – Security Logging

    _____ – Logging Options

Current Version Date: 07/27/2011

_____ – Logging File Options

_____ – ICMP

    _____ – Allow incoming request

    _____ – Allow incoming time request

    _____ – Allow incoming router request

    _____ – Allow outgoing destination unreachable

    _____ – Allow outgoing source quench

    _____ – Allow outgoing parameter problem

    _____ – Allow outgoing time exceeded

    _____ – Allow redirect

    _____ – Allow outgoing packet too big

Current Version Date: 07/27/2011

Lab #4 – Assessment Worksheet

Implement Organizational-Wide Network and WLAN Access Controls

Course Name & Number: _____

Student Name: _____

Instructor Name: _____

Lab Due Date: _____

Overview

In this lab, the students will enable and configure internal host-based Windows Server and Workstation firewalls. They use their own "Student" and "TargetWindows01" VMs to test their own internal host-based firewall configurations. They also perform Wireless LAN research and review Wireless LAN (WLAN) security standards from NIST and IASE documents. Students will identify security controls and access controls for both wired and wireless LANs within the LAN Domain.

Lab Assessment Questions & Answers

1. What risk exposure are you subjecting your Microsoft Windows systems to by opening up ports on your internal firewall?

2. Using the VM's on your student workstation, how can you test if your Windows internal firewall is configured properly?

3. Name at least three significant risks of logging in to access points in airports, hotels and other public places. Explain.

4. Name at least three WLAN network devices commonly found in enterprise WLAN systems.

5. Name at least 5 methods of wireless communications that need to be secured and accounted for in a typical enterprise environment?

6. How does Bluetooth communication differ from a regular WLAN with access points and clients?

7. What are the risks involved in having the wired and wireless NICs enabled simultaneously on a laptop or workstation?

Current Version Date: 07/27/2011

8. What is the major reason why WEP encryption is not suitable for securing a WLAN connection? What is recommended for use with WLAN infrastructures?

9. What is a Man-in-the-Middle Attack? Explain.

10. What is a Network Injection Attack? Explain.

Current Version Date: 07/27/2011

Laboratory #5

Lab #5: Enhance Security Controls for Access to Sensitive Data

Learning Objectives and Outcomes

Upon completing this lab, students will be able to complete the following tasks:

- Define proper access controls for employees, contractors, and third-parties in accordance with defined access control policy definition

- Identify best practices for conducting interviews and background checks to mitigate the risk within the User Domain

- Describe best practices regarding hiring, job rotations, and separation of duties to mitigate the risk within the User Domain

- Apply best practices within acceptable use policies and confidentiality agreements to mitigate the risk within the User Domain

- Implement best practices for minimizing employee exposure to sensitive data such as employee security awareness training, encryption, or sanitization of data where appropriate

Required Setup and Tools

This is a paper-based lab.

The standard lab computer with Microsoft Office 2007 or higher and Adobe Acrobat PDF Reader is required for this lab. Students will need to review the seven domains of a typical IT infrastructure diagram (Figure 3), work together in groups, and answer the Lab #5 – Assessment Worksheet using Microsoft Word.

Recommended Procedures

Lab #5 – Student Steps

Students should perform the following steps:

1. Download and review the DoD document provided by IASE for DISA called Access Control in Support of Information Systems:

   http://iase.disa.mil/stigs/stig/access_control_stig_v2r2_final_26_dec_2008.pdf

2. Investigate the following Access Control Layers:

   a. The Access Control Perimeter

   b. Asset Containers

Current Version Date: 07/27/2011

    c.   Workplace Perimeter

3.   Investigate Access Control Methods and Technical Strategies

    a.   Identification, Authentication and Authorization

    b.   Logical Access Controls

        i.   Network Architecture Controls

        ii.   Remote Network Access

        iii.   Security Network Ports

        iv.   Encryption

        v.   PKI Compliance Requirements

        vi.   Passwords, PINs, and Implementations of "Something You Know"

    c.   Physical Access Controls

        i.   Classified Storage and Handling

        ii.   Badges, Memory Cards and Smart Cards

        iii.   Physical Tokens and Physical Intrusion Detection Systems

4.   Investigate the following Access Control Integration and Administrative Strategies:

    a.   Biometric Systems

    b.   Separation of Duties

    c.   Protecting the Enrollment Process

    d.   Protecting the Verification Process

    e.   Cryptographic Controls

    f.   Risk Analysis

    g.   Integrating Access Control Methods

5.   Investigate the following Key Infrastructure (PKI):

    a.   DoD Approved PKI

    b.   Multi-factor Authentication

    c.   Identification and authentication through digital signature of a challenge

    d.   Data integrity through digital signature of the information

    e.   Confidentiality through encryption

    f.   Assists with technical non-repudiation through digital signatures

6.   Investigate these concepts on mitigating risk in the User Domain:

    a.   Interviewing and background screening

    b.   Hiring, job rotations, and separation of duties

    c.   Security Policies

Current Version Date: 07/27/2011

7. Discuss how to implement the following:

   a. Acceptable Use Policies

   b. Confidentiality Agreements

   c. Non-compete agreements

   d. Best practices for minimizing employee exposure to sensitive data

   e. New employee orientation training

   f. On-going Security Awareness training

Deliverables

Upon completion of Lab #5: Enhance Security Controls for Access to Sensitive Data, students are required to provide the following deliverables:

1. Lab #5 – Develop a chart listing at least 5 Technical Controls and 5 Administrative Controls that are required for properly implementing access controls throughout an IT infrastructure. Include a description of the controls for each after the chart, explaining why, in your opinion, these are critical access controls to implement. Please keep this report under 500 words.

2. Lab #5 – Lab Assessment Questions & Answers

Evaluation Criteria and Rubrics

The following are the evaluation criteria and rubrics for Lab #5 that the students must perform:

1. Was the student able to define proper access controls for employees, contractors, and third-parties in accordance with defined access control policy definition? – [**20%**]

2. Was the student able to identify best practices for performing interviews and background checks to mitigate the risk within the User Domain? – [**20%**]

3. Was the student able to describe best practices regarding hiring, job rotations, and separation of duties to mitigate the risk within the User Domain? – [**20%**]

4. Was the student able to apply best practices within acceptable use policies and confidentiality agreements to mitigate the risk within the User Domain? – [**20%**]

5. Was the student able to implement best practices for minimizing employee exposure to sensitive data such as employee security awareness training, encryption, or sanitization of data where appropriate? – [**20%**]

Current Version Date: 07/27/2011

Lab #5 – Assessment Worksheet

Enhance Security Controls for Access to Sensitive Data

Course Name & Number: _____

Student Name: _____

Instructor Name: _____

Lab Due Date: _____

Overview

The student will enhance security controls by controlling access to sensitive data and reviewing best practices for maintain security in the User Domain. To do this, he/she will download a Best Practices document called a STIG from the DoD website provided by IASE a division of DISA. The Access Control document reviews all the possible logical and physical controls required to properly secure and classify data through identification, authentication and authorization. The student will develop a chart listing at least 5 Technical Controls and 5 Administrative Controls that are required for properly implementing access control in the User Domain. Include a description of how each security control mitigates the risk exposure within the User Domain.

Lab Assessment Questions & Answers

1. What are the three major categories used to provide authentication of an individual?

2. What is Authorization and how is this concept aligned with Identification and Authentication?

Current Version Date: 07/27/2011

3. Provide at least 3 examples of Network Architecture Controls that help enforce data access policies at the LAN-to-WAN Domain level.

4. When a computer is physically connected to a network port, manual procedures and/or an automated method must exist to perform what type of security functions at the Network Port and Data Switch level for access control? Name and define at least three.

5. What is a Network Access Control (NAC) System? Explain its benefits in securing access control to a network.

6. Explain the purpose of a Public Key Infrastructure (PKI) and give an example of how you would implement it in a large organization whose major concern is the proper distribution of certificates across many sites.

Current Version Date: 07/27/2011

7. PKI provides the capabilities of digital signatures and encryption to implement what security services? Name at least three.

8. What is the X.509 standard and how does it relate to PKI?

9. What is the difference between Identification and Verification in regard to Biometric Access Controls?

10. Provide a written explanation of what implementing Separation of Duties would look like in regard to managing a PKI Infrastructure for a large organization.

11. What are the 3 categories of vulnerability severity codes?

Current Version Date: 07/27/2011

12. True or False. The use of 802.11i configured to use AES encryption, 802.1X authentication services along with the Extensible Authentication Protocol (EAP) provides the best solution for the enterprise level WLAN, particularly a high security environment.

13. True or False. It is a best practice to write a password down and store it near the vicinity of the computer for easy access.

14. True or False. From a security perspective, biometric verification is best deployed as a component of two-factor or three-factor authentication.

15. From an access control security perspective, why is performing an asset valuation or alignment to a data classification standard the first step in designing proper security controls?

Current Version Date: 07/27/2011

Laboratory #6

Lab #6: Enhance Security Controls Leveraging Group Policy Objects

Learning Objectives and Outcomes

Upon completing this lab, the students will be able to complete the following tasks:

- Design a layered access control list schema for file system access based on users, groups and applications, and Group Policy Objects

- Apply User Rights Assignments to Group Policy Objects enforcing time zones, application restrictions, backup and encryption options

- Align proper access controls for the three states of data within an information system by aligning read-write-delete access rights to different file types as per data owner permission requirements

- Define appropriate access control rights for end-users, system administrators, and super-user account privileges based on a data classification standard

- Implement access control best practices for Windows Active Directory and user access control features for Windows servers and workstation

Required Setup and Tools

This lab requires that the instructor and student workstations and VMs be connected to the shared, classroom layer 2 switch and physically disconnected from the classroom/building network and public Internet. This will also allow the Instructor to enable the shared, DHCP server to be used for all the VMs used in this equipment-based lab.

NOTE: The instructor will enable the lab's DHCP server by powering on the "DHCPWindows01" server which will allocate a source IP host address to all workstations and VMs enabled. Only 1 DHCP server should be enabled for IP host address allocation on the same IP subnetwork at a given time.

The following equipment is required for this equipment-based lab:

A) Student classroom workstations (with at least 2GB RAM) capable of supporting the removable hard drive with the VM server farm and up to 2 simultaneously running VMs.

NOTE: Only one VM will be running at full speed on a workstation with only 2GB of RAM. If you power-on 2 VMs at once on a workstation with only 2GB of RAM, there will be performance slowdown. For optimal performance, load 2 or more VMs with at least 4GB of RAM in your workstation.

Current Version Date: 07/27/2011

B) Instructor workstations (with at least 4 Gig RAM) that shall act as the Instructor's demo lab workstation. The instructor will display the Instructor VM or other Server Farm VMs on the LCD projector to demo the loading and configuring of the VM Server Farm and execute demonstrations of the equipment-based labs using VMware Player.

C) Student workstations will use their own VM Server Farm. VMware Player will be used to run the VMs on both Instructor and Student workstations. It is strongly recommended that the VMs be copied to the local classroom workstation whenever possible to improve performance.

The following summarizes the setup, configuration, and equipment needed to perform Lab #6: "TargetWindows01" is a Windows 2003 Standard Server VM used with VM Server Farm v2. "TargetWindows02" is a newer Windows 2008 Standard Server VM that was released as an upgrade to VM Server Farm v2. "TargetWindows02" VM is now part of the VM Server Farm v3.

Although the "TargetWindows02" 2008 Server is not mandatory to perform this equipment-based lab, it is a more up to date VM to be performing this equipment-based lab.

1. The VM Server Farm (Version 2 or higher) with the following VMs:
    a. A Target Windows 2003 Standard Server VM ("TargetWindows01"); or
    b. A Target Windows 2008 Standard Server VM ("TargetWindows02")

2. A standard classroom workstation must have the following software applications loaded to perform this lab:
    a. VMware Player 3.x
    b. Microsoft Office 2007 or higher for Lab Assessment Questions & Answers

Recommended Procedures

Equipment-Based Lab #6 – Student Steps:

Students should perform the following steps:

1. Connect your removable hard drive to your classroom workstation

NOTE: The "DHCPWindows01" server and the "InstructorVM" are not required for a demonstration of this lab. Instead, a static IP address **MUST** be applied to the Target Windows Server prior to running the "dcpromo" command for proper DNS and Domain Controller configuration.

Current Version Date: 07/27/2011

2. Power-on only **ONE** of the following Target Windows Servers available in the VM server farm:

    a. "TargetWindows01" **OR** "TargetWindows02"

3. Target Windows Server Logons and Computer Information is as follows:

    a. Usernames: "administrator", "instructor". OR "student" (without quotes)

    b. Password: "ISS316Security" (without quotes, case sensitive)

    c. Target Windows Servers available in the Mock IT Server Farm Version 3:

       • "TargetWindows01": Windows Server 2003 Standard Edition 32-bit

       • "TargetWindows02": Windows Server 2008 Standard Edition 32-bit

4. Launch Active Directory Users and Computers on Target Windows Server: Start -> Administrative Tools -> Active Directory Users and Computers

5. In the treeview, expand Forest -> Domains -> domainname -> right click Properties

6. Select the 'Group Policy Objects' tab and right-mouse-click on Group Policy Objects

7. Use the GPOs created in Lab #1 to customize and add User Rights Assignment to the following four GPOs:

    a. Inspector General

    b. Federal Acquisition Regulation (FAR)

    c. Awarded Contracts

    d. Senate Chairs

8. Ensure that the assigned users are part of its corresponding groups and GPO

    a. Select the GPO and click 'Properties'

    b. Select the 'Security' tab and ensure that the appropriate users are listed under 'Groups or usernames'

9. Under Policies on each of the GPOs find User Rights Assignments

10. Assign at least one group appropriate application restriction to each GPO

11. Users should have appropriate access rights and permissions to the data they require

12. Software Restriction Policies allow you to setup which application the users can open. To create or edit a software restriction GPO

    a. Select the GPO under Group Policy in the domain's properties window

    b. Select 'Edit' to go into the Group Policy Object Editor

    c. Expand User Configuration -> Windows Settings -> Security Settings -> 'Software Restrictions'

    d. Edit or Add new object by clicking the 'Action' tab at the top

Current Version Date: 07/27/2011

13. Provide remote access considerations provided for Senate Chairs and Inspector General Users

    a. Select the "GPO" under Group Policy in the domain's property window

    b. Click 'Edit' to go into the Group Policy Object Editor

    c. Expand Computer Configuration -> Windows Settings -> Security Settings -> Local Policies -> User Rights Assignments

    d. Double click 'Allow log on through Terminal Services'

    e. Select the checkbox 'Define these policy settings'

    f. Click the 'Add User or Group' button

    g. Enter the group "GPO" and click "Ok".

    h. Press 'Ok' again to save this policy under the corresponding GPO

14. For Senate Chairs group members consider/implement access time restrictions considered for users and international locations

    a. Select the "GPO" under Group Policy in the domain's property window

    b. Click 'Edit' to go into the Group Policy Object Editor

    c. Expand Computer Configuration -> Windows Settings -> Security Settings -> Local Policies -> Security Options

    d. Double click 'Microsoft network server: Disconnect clients when logon hours expire"

    e. Now we must set the log on times for the corresponding Group by going to the Active Directory User and Computers window (Start -> Administrative Tools -> Active Directory Users and Computers)

        ▪ Under the domain, select Users and Right Click the user Account

        ▪ Select the 'Account' Tab

        ▪ Click 'Logon Hours' button to set the logon times for this user

15. Give/provide considerations for backup and recovery for all groups

    a. To backup GPOs, go to the Group Policy Management Console (Start -> Administrative Tools -> Group Policy Management

        ▪ Expand the domain -> Group Policy Objects

        ▪ Right click the desired "GPO" and select 'Backup'

        ▪ Specify a location to save the GPO backup and give an appropriate description

        ▪ Select 'Backup' and repeat steps for all desired GPOs

16. Show a screenshot of what policies you would set if you were to consider encryption on some/all of the file systems

Current Version Date: 07/27/2011

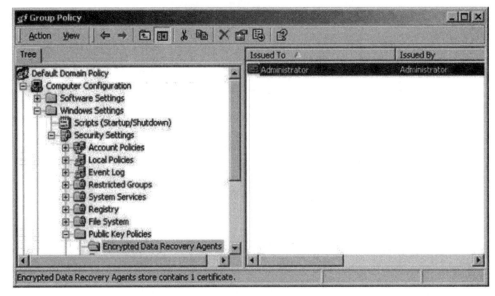

Figure 4 – GPO Encryption Policies

17. Build a matrix to identify the common needs of each data file, application and user

18. Build GPOs to group access and rights requirements

19. Provide screenshots of the User Rights Assignments and Policy Settings chosen for each of the four GPOs

Deliverables

Upon completion of Lab #6: Enhance Security Controls Leveraging Group Policy Objects, students are required to provide the following deliverables:

1. Lab #6 – Lab deliverables include screen captures of the GPO's and user rights settings implemented in the equipment-based lab

2. Lab #6 – Lab Assessment Questions & Answers

Evaluation Criteria and Rubrics

The following are the evaluation criteria and rubrics for Lab #6 that the students must perform:

- Was the student able to design a layered access control list schema for file system access based on users, groups and applications, and Group Policy Objects? – [**20%**]

- Was the student able to apply User Rights Assignments to Group Policy Objects enforcing time zones, application restrictions, backup and encryption options? – [**20%**]

Current Version Date: 07/27/2011

- Was the student able to align proper access controls for the three states of data within an information system by aligning read-write-delete access rights to different file types as per data owner permission requirements? – **[20%]**

- Was the student able to define appropriate access control rights for end-users, system administrators, and super-user account privileges based on a data classification standard? – **[20%]**

- Was the student able to implement access control best practices for Windows Active Directory and user access control features for Windows servers and workstation? – **[20%]**

Current Version Date: 07/27/2011

Lab #6 – Assessment Worksheet

Enhance Security Controls Leveraging Group Policy Objects

Course Name & Number: _____

Student Name: _____

Instructor Name: _____

Lab Due Date: _____

Overview

This lab is an extension of Lab #1 and includes additional security access controls that can be enabled within Applications and Groups in the created Group Policy Objects. Using the user accounts and group definitions created in Lab #1, the students will apply user rights based on user group definitions and GPOs. They will also define encryption options, data backup and recovery strategies necessary to enhance the security controls defined by policy statements. They will also configure the access controls and restrictions to accommodate users from different time zones and international users.

Lab Assessment Questions & Answers

1. What are the available Password Policy options that could be enforced to improve security in a Group Policy Object?

2. How would you set security permissions and user access rights on a home computer using Windows XP Professional or similar that is not a member of the domain?

Current Version Date: 07/27/2011

3. Why is the use of the different password policy options available and why is it important to implement complexity and length requirements?

4. Microsoft defines user rights in two types of categories: Logon Rights and Privileges. Explain the difference of the two from an access control perspective.

5. Name at least 5 Logon Rights and 5 Privileges available in Microsoft GPOs.

6. Which privileges in a GPO can override permissions set on an object?

7. What are the benefits of User Rights Assignments in your own words used as security controls and deployed across a domain of servers and workstations?

Current Version Date: 07/27/2011

8. Explain why you would have to create a service account for applications and assign them elevated privileges with a GPO. Present a well thought out argument as to the danger, from the security perspective, in creating service accounts for applications and what can be done to mitigate the risk.

9. Provide at least 3 examples of either Rights or Privileges typically required by a service account in the User Rights Assignments section of a GPO.

10. Provide an explanation of why restricting access based on time zones or international users helps organizations achieve C-I-A as required by the Senate Chairs Group Policy Object definition? Assume Senate Chairs Group provides 24 x 7 x 365 customer service support in different time zones.

Current Version Date: 07/27/2011

Laboratory #7

Lab #7: Design a Multi-factor Authentication Process

Learning Objectives and Outcomes

Upon completing this lab, students will be able to complete the following tasks:

- Align appropriate authentication requirements to different data types according to a Data Classification Standard

- Define requirements for remote access from the Internet for the LAN-to-WAN Domain

- Align best practices for private sector and public sector authentication requirements that support online applications such as e-commerce, online banking, and online government

- Recommend best practices for remote access security measures and multi-factor authentication for employees and contractors through the public Internet

- Design a proper authentication solution using a RADIUS and TACACs+ authentication server solution as well as IEEE 802.11 WLAN infrastructures

Required Setup and Tools

This is a paper-based lab.

A classroom workstation with a live Internet connection, Microsoft Office 2007 or higher, and Adobe PDF Reader is required for this lab.

Recommended Procedures

Lab #7 – Student Steps:

Students should perform the following steps:

1. Browse to and open the FFIEC Authentication Guidance for Internet Banking:

   http://www.ffiec.gov/pdf/authentication_guidance.pdf

2. Investigate the following requirements for an Information Security Program:

   a. Identifies and assesses the risks associated with Internet-based products and services

   b. Identifies risk mitigation actions, including appropriate authentication strength

   c. Measures and evaluates customer awareness efforts

3. Investigate the following Recommended Risk Assessment Process:

   a. Identify all transactions and levels of access associated with Internet-based customer products and services

Current Version Date: 07/27/2011

   b.   Identify and assess the risk mitigation techniques, including authentication methodologies, employed for each transaction type and level of access

   c.   Include the ability to gauge the effectiveness of risk mitigation techniques for current and changing risk factors for each transaction type and level of access.

4.   Browse to the IASE/DISA STIGs website: http://iase.disa.mil/stigs/stig/index.html

5.   Download the following Secure Remote Computing Guideline Documents/ZIP File: unclassified_secure_remote_computing_v2r3_stig_20100827.zip

6.   Extract the.ZIP file and browse to the unzipped directory.

7.   Open the U_SRC_V2R3_Overview.pdf, this reviews the potential vulnerabilities and configuration recommendations for secure remote access as per DoD guidelines.

8.   Investigate the following concepts from this overarching DoD standards document for secure remote access:

   a.   Security Recommendations for Remote Access and Telework

   b.   Assessment, Enforcement and Remediation Services

   c.   Endpoint Security

   d.   Security Readiness Review Requirements

9.   Investigate the following Remote Access security checklist and guideline document on DoD requirements for Remote Access: U_Remote_Access_Policy_V2R3_STIG.pdf

   a.   Vulnerability Key: V0019834

      i.   Remote Privileged Access

10.   Browse to and open the TACACs+ and RADIUS Comparison by Cisco Systems: http://www.cisco.com/application/pdf/paws/13838/10.pdf

11.   Research and Compare TACACS+ and RADIUS in the following areas:

   a.   UDP and TCP

   b.   Packet Encryption

   c.   Authentication and Authorization

   d.   Multiprotocol Support

   e.   Router Management

   f.   Interoperability

   g.   Traffic

   h.   Device Support

Current Version Date: 07/27/2011

Deliverables

Upon completion of Lab #7: Design a Multi-factor Authentication Process, the students are required to provide the following deliverables:

1. Lab #7 – Develop a chart listing the remote access requirements for an online banking and e-commerce web solution using a multi-factor authentication plan
2. Lab #7 – Lab Assessment Questions & Answers

Evaluation Criteria and Rubrics

The following are the evaluation criteria and rubrics for Lab #7 that the students must demonstrate:

- Was the student able to align appropriate authentication requirements to different data types according to a Data Classification Standard? – **[20%]**
- Was the student able to define requirements for remote access from the Internet for the LAN-to-WAN Domain? – **[20%]**
- Was the student able to align best practices for private sector and public sector authentication requirements that support online applications such as e-commerce, online banking, and online government? – **[20%]**
- Was the student able to recommend best practices for remote access security measures and multi-factor authentication for employees and contractors through the public Internet? – **[20%]**
- Was the student able to design a proper authentication solution using a RADIUS and TACACs+ authentication server solution as well as IEEE 802.11 WLAN infrastructures? – **[20%]**

Current Version Date: 07/27/2011

Lab #7 – Assessment Worksheet

Design a Multi-factor Authentication Process

Course Name & Number: _____

Student Name: _____

Instructor Name: _____

Lab Due Date: _____

Overview

Students will research best practices for private sector and public sector authentication as it relates to e-commerce and on-line banking. Then they will research the best practices for remote access for employees through public Internet and for employees of city, county, state, and federal governments, based on DoD standards for secure remote access. Multi-factor authentication and restrictions based on data types and sensitivity according to Data Classification Standards were discussed in previous labs and should be taken into consideration when investigating the use of RADIUS, TACACs+ and WLAN authentication methodologies.

Lab Assessment Questions & Answers

1. In an Internet Banking Financial Institution is Single Factor Authentication acceptable? Why or why not?

Current Version Date: 07/27/2011

2. Explain the difference between Positive Verification and Negative Verification.

3. What vulnerabilities are introduced by implementing a Remote Access Server?

4. What is a recommended best practice when implementing a Remote Access Policy server user authentication service?

5. Name at least 3 remote access protections or security controls that must be in place to provide secure remote access.

Current Version Date: 07/27/2011

6. When dealing with RADIUS and TACACS+ for authentication methods, what protocols are used at Layer 4 for each of these techniques?

7. In TACACS+ communications, what part of the packet gets encrypted and which part is clear text?

8. In RADIUS authentication, what is the purpose of the "Authenticator"?

9. Which of these two, RADIUS and TACACS+, combines both authentication and authorization?

10. Is combining authentication and authorization a less or more robust way of handling authentication? Explain.

Current Version Date: 07/27/2011

11. True or False. Access controls consisting of login credentials with a userid and password is considered two-factor authentication.

12. Which of the following authentication solutions is more robust and provides a greater level of secure authentication for remote access and mobile users: Login/Password, RADIUS, TACACS+ ?

13. True or False. Providing and entering a WLAN SSID is like a form of single-factor authentication to connect to a WLAN.

14. True or False. An online banking system requires that the user enter a second password via a token or SmartCard device. When entering your second password the token or SmartCard transmit a real-time password that the user must enter to gain access to their online banking account. This is an example of strong, two-factor authentication.

15. True or False. An e-commerce website that uses HTTP:// for single-factor authentication (i.e., login credentials) is secure through the public Internet.

Current Version Date: 07/27/2011

Laboratory #8

Lab #8: Align Appropriate PKI Solutions Based on Remote Access and Data Sensitivity

Learning Objectives and Outcomes

Upon completing this lab, students will be able to complete the following tasks:

- Identify solutions for remote access using PKI according to defined access controls and data classification standard requirements

- Design a layered remote access PKI solution that is based on the type of user and the type of data being accessed

- Compare and contrast PKI solutions for identification, authentication and authorization from security operations and management perspectives

- Identify the strengths and weaknesses within each type of encryption after a thorough comparison and analysis of pros and cons

- Align secure remote access protocols (IP-SEC, VPN, TLS, SSL, SSH, etc.) with different business application requirements and PKI capabilities

Required Setup and Tools

This is a paper-based lab.

A classroom workstation with a live Internet connection, Microsoft Office 2007 or higher, and Adobe PDF Reader is required for this lab.

Recommended Procedures

Lab #8 – Student Steps:

Students should perform the following steps:

1. Conduct research on the following topics using Google:
    a. Encryption
    b. Public key infrastructure
    c. Data privacy
    d. Data security

2. Compare and contrast the two major classes of encryption and hashing
    a. Symmetric
    b. Asymmetric

Current Version Date: 07/27/2011

    c.   Hash

3.   Research the Primary Components of PKI Solutions

    a.   Certificate Authorities

    b.   Web of Trust

    c.   Temporary Certificates & Single Sign-On

    d.   Simple public key infrastructure

4.   Compare Three Different Commercial PKI Solutions

    a.   Entrust http://www.entrust.com/

    b.   Public Key Infrastructure for Windows Server 2003 http://technet.microsoft.com/en-us/library/cc772670%28WS.10%29.aspx

    c.   RSA Certificate Manager http://www.rsa.com/node.aspx?id=1224

5.   Investigate how PKI is leveraged with different protocols

    a.   VPNs and Public Key Infrastructure

        http://onlamp.com/pub/a/security/2004/09/23/vpns_and_pki.html

    b.   Deploying a Public Key Infrastructure with OpenSSL

        http://www.oreillynet.com/pub/a/security/2004/10/21/vpns_and_pki.html

    c.   Cisco Digital Certificates PKI for IPSec VPNs

        https://learningnetwork.cisco.com/servlet/JiveServlet/downloadBody/3592-102-1-9755/Digital%20Certificates%20PKI%20for%20IPSec%20VPNs.pdf

6.   Research Private vs. Public Sector PKI Requirements to incorporate in written analysis

    a.   Federal Public Key Infrastructure Policy Authority http://www.idmanagement.gov/fpkipa/

    b.   NIST Public Key Infrastructures

        http://csrc.nist.gov/groups/ST/crypto_apps_infra/pki/index.html

    c.   PKI Policy Bodies and Other Authentication Frameworks http://www.oasis-pki.org/resources/policies/

Deliverables

Upon completion of Lab #8: Align Appropriate PKI Solutions Based on Remote Access and Data Sensitivity, the students are required to provide the following deliverables:

1.   Lab #8 – Develop a 3-5 page Summary of Findings report that discusses and highlights your research on Private vs. Public Sector PKI Requirements focusing on the following topics:

    a.   The purpose, benefits, drawbacks, and methods of encryption identifying the major classification of encryption algorithms as symmetric, asymmetric or hashing.

Current Version Date: 07/27/2011

      b.   Data Classification and Sensitivity Considerations

      c.   Incorporate digital signatures and block ciphers into the research summary

      d.   Secure Remote Access Recommendations

2. Lab #8 – Assessment Worksheet Questions & Answers

Evaluation Criteria and Rubrics

The following are the evaluation criteria and rubrics for Lab #8 that the students must perform:

- Was the student able to identify solutions for remote access using PKI according to defined access controls and data classification standard requirements? – **[20%]**

- Was the student able to design a layered remote access PKI solution that is based on the type of user and the type of data being accessed? – **[20%]**

- Was the student able to compare and contrast PKI solutions for identification, authentication and authorization from security operations and management perspectives? – **[20%]**

- Was the student able to identify the strengths and weaknesses within each type of encryption after a thorough comparison and analysis of pros and cons? – **[20%]**

- Was the student able to align secure remote access protocols (IP-SEC, VPN, TLS, SSL, SSH, etc.) with different business application requirements and PKI capabilities? – **[20%]**

Current Version Date: 07/27/2011

Lab #8 – Assessment Worksheet

Align Appropriate PKI Solutions Based on Remote Access and Data Sensitivity

Course Name & Number: _____

Student Name: _____

Instructor Name: _____

Lab Due Date: _____

Overview

The student will research several PKI concepts and solutions that are based on the resources provided in the lab and online. The student will assess the appropriate role for PKI as it relates to remote access rights on classified data, based on the role of the user and the sensitivity of the data. The student will also review how to integrate PKI authentication into such technologies and protocols as IP-SEC, VPN, SSL and others, while taking into consideration both the private and public sector organizations. After creating the written analysis of encryption methods evaluating their benefits, roles and limitations, answer these assessment questions.

Lab Assessment Questions & Answers

1. Where can you store your public keys or public certificate files in the public domain? Is this the same thing as a Public Key Infrastructure (KI) server?

2. What do you need to do if you want to decrypt encrypted messages and files from a trusted sender?

Current Version Date: 07/27/2011

3. When referring to IPSec tunnel mode, what two types of headers are available and how do they differ?

4. Provide a step by step progression for a typical Certificate Enrollment process with a Certificate Authority.

5. When designing a PKI infrastructure what are the advantages and disadvantages of making the CA available publicly over the Internet or keeping it within the private network?

6. Designing a PKI involves several steps. Per the Windows Best Practices for Designing a PKI, what are those steps? In your own words, explain what each step is meant to do.

Current Version Date: 07/27/2011

7. When deploying a PKI, it is important to understand how many CAs will be necessary to properly implement the infrastructure. Provide 3-5 important considerations that must be taken into account before deploying a PKI for a large environment.

8. What is the main function of the certutil.exe command line tool available in Microsoft Windows?

9. What is the OpenSSL project and their mission?

10. What is the purpose of Single Sign-on? Provide one example of how it benefits security and one example as to how it can increase security risk.

Current Version Date: 07/27/2011

11. True or False. You can enable VPN technology for remote access for mobile workers using the public Internet and also for Wireless LANs (WLAN) within the LAN Domain to ensure confidentiality.

12. Relate back to the C-I-A tenets of information systems security. Hashing provides file _____ while encryption provides file _____.

13. Which method of hashing provides for stronger file integrity verification and why? MD5 or SHA-1?

14. True or False. By Public Key Infrastructure, it is acceptable to share and host your public key for all to see and use on a public or shared key server.

15. True or False. You can host your public key at http://pgp.mit.edu/ because MIT hosts a Public Key Infrastructure for all to use.

Current Version Date: 07/27/2011

Laboratory #9

Lab #9: Apply Encryption to Mitigate Risk Exposure

Learning Objectives and Outcomes

Upon completing this lab, students will be able to complete the following tasks:

- Identify a Public Key Infrastructure (PKI) solution that can help ensure the confidentiality of business communications

- Implement non-repudiation and the use of digital signatures when transmitting sensitive data over public and private networks

- Describe the role and the major components of a Certificate Authority (CA) in supporting an enterprise with a PKI environment and secure business communications

- Identify and compare open-source cryptography and encryption solutions to mitigate the risk from clear-text data and data transmissions

- Apply appropriate cryptography and encryption techniques for different data states and the type of protection available to protect each data state

Required Setup and Tools

This lab requires that the instructor and student workstations and VMs be connected to the shared, classroom layer 2 switch and physically disconnected from the classroom/building network and public Internet. This will also allow the Instructor to enable the shared, DHCP server to be used for all the VMs used in this equipment-based lab.

> **NOTE:** The instructor will enable the lab's DHCP server by powering on the "DHCPWindows01" server which will allocate a source IP host address to all workstations and VMs enabled. Only 1 DHCP server should be enabled for IP host address allocation on the same IP subnetwork at a given time.

The following equipment is required for this equipment-based lab:

A) Student classroom workstations (with at least 2GB RAM) capable of supporting the removable hard drive with the VM server farm and up to 2 simultaneously running VMs.

Current Version Date: 07/27/2011

NOTE: Only one VM will be running at full speed on a workstation with only 2GB of RAM. If you power-on 2 VMs at once on a workstation with only 2GB of RAM, there will be performance slowdown. For optimal performance, load 2 or more VMs with at least 4GB of RAM in your workstation.

B) Instructor workstations (with at least 4 Gig RAM) that shall act as the Instructor's demo lab workstation. The instructor will display the Instructor VM or other Server Farm VMs on the LCD projector to demo the loading and configuring of the VM Server Farm and execute demonstrations of the equipment-based labs using VMware Player.

C) Student workstations will use their own VM Server Farm. VMware Player will be used to run the VMs on both Instructor and Student workstations. It is strongly recommended that the VMs be copied to the local classroom workstation whenever possible to improve performance.

The following summarizes the setup, configuration, and equipment needed to perform Lab #9: "TargetWindows01" is a Windows 2003 Standard Server VM used with VM Server Farm v2. "TargetWindows02" is a newer Windows 2008 Standard Server VM that was released as an upgrade to VM Server Farm v2. "TargetWindows02" VM is now part of the VM Server Farm v3.

Although the "TargetWindows02" 2008 Server is not mandatory to perform this equipment-based lab, it is a more up to date VM to be performing this equipment-based lab.

1. The VM Server Farm (Version 2 or higher) with the following VMs:
   a. A Target Windows 2003 Standard Server VM ("TargetWindows01"); or
   b. A Target Windows 2008 Standard Server VM ("TargetWindows02")
2. A standard classroom workstation must have the following software applications loaded to perform this lab:
   c. VMware Player 3.x
   d. Microsoft Office 2007 or higher for Lab Assessment Questions & Answers

Recommended Procedures

Equipment-Based Lab #9 – Student Steps

Students should perform the following steps:

1. Connect your removable hard drive to your classroom workstation
2. Boot up your Student VM and Microsoft DHCP VM server to allocate IP host address

Current Version Date: 07/27/2011

3. Enable your DOS command prompt (Start -> Run -> 'cmd') and type "ipconfig" and "ping" your allocated IP host address 172.30.0.__ , the DHCP server 172.30.0.10, and the IP default gateway router 172.30.0.1

4. Login to your Student VM using the following credentials:

    a. Login ID: "student" (case sensitive)

    b. Password: "ISS316Security" (case sensitive)

5. Verify that GPG is pre-installed as an application. If it is not then look in the \ITT_Tools\ or "\ISSA_Tools\ folder on your vWorkstation for the GPG install file and run the installation

6. To open the program, click on "GPG desktop program" and a prompt to create your private key will appear

7. Insert the name "PKIUser" or <Your Name> as the name asked for. Click "forward"

8. Insert an email, i.e. "student@vlabsolutions.com", and click "forward"

9. Ensure you create a backup copy of your new key when prompted and click "forward"

10. Enter a passphrase "Accesscontrols" to further encrypt your newly created key

---

NOTE: Please use "Accesscontrols" as the passphrase as it will be need to be used to decrypt and encrypt messages. Whatever you use as the passphrase, do NOT forget what it is and write it down.

---

11. After generating the secret key, save it to the desktop so you can find it later

12. Click on "close", and now open up GPG again. Highlight the key you created, click on the export option, and name the key "PKIUser1" or <Your Name>, as appropriate

13. Power-on only ONE of the following Target Windows Servers available in the VM server farm: "TargetWindows01" OR "TargetWindows02" (pause the Instructor/Student VM if necessary)

14. Target Windows Server Logons and Computer Information is as follows:

    a. Usernames: "administrator", "instructor". OR "student" (without quotes)

    b. Password: "ISS316Security" (without quotes, case sensitive)

15. Perform steps 6-13 on the Target Windows Server using a different name like "PKIUser2"

16. Transfer both sets of keys to each of the VMs using external HDD or a shared VM folder; ensure that both public keys are on both VMs

17. Use import button and import keys to both VMs

18. On your Student VM, right click newly imported key. Click on "Set owner trust" option, and set it to "full" in the options

19. On your Student VM, right click the newly imported key. Click on the "Sign keys" option

Current Version Date: 07/27/2011

20. Enter your secret key passphrase ("Accesscontrols") from previous step to sign the public key to your secret keyring as "authorized"

21. Repeat steps 19 and 21 on the "TargetWindows01" or "TargetWindows02" VM Server

22. For Hashing, we can verify the public key imported in each VM matches the Fingerprint in the GPG home window

23. On your Student VM, create a new file on the desktop using notepad. Name the file "encryptme.txt" and add a message to your liking in the text file

24. Once a file is created and saved, you can right click, and chose the sign and encrypt option

25. Be sure that you check the "remove unencrypted file" option at the bottom

26. Add both certificates to the options and click "encrypt"

27. Once a file is encrypted, you will see the encrypted file replace the plain text file on the desktop, right click and choose "decrypt/verify" option

28. Now transfer the encrypted file to the Target Windows Server's desktop, "right click the file" on the VM and select "decrypt the file" on the other system

29. Secure file decryption using the provided encryption keys has now been successfully performed

Deliverables

Upon completion of Lab #9: Apply Encryption to Mitigate Risk Exposure, the students are required to provide the following deliverables:

1. Lab #9 – Download open-source encryption software and install it on your Student VM and generate both a public and private key (passphrase generate)

2. Lab #9 – Lab Assessment Questions & Answers

Evaluation Criteria and Rubrics

The following are the evaluation criteria and rubrics for Lab #9 that the students must perform:

- Was the student able to identify a Public Key Infrastructure (PKI) solution that can help ensure the confidentiality of business communications? – [**20%**]

- Was the student able to implement non-repudiation and the use of digital signatures when transmitting sensitive data over public and private networks? – [**20%**]

- Was the student able to describe the role and the major components of a Certificate Authority (CA) in supporting an enterprise with a PKI environment and secure business communications? – [**20%**]

Current Version Date: 07/27/2011

- Was the student able to identify and compare open-source cryptography and encryption solutions to mitigate the risk from clear-text data and data transmissions? – [**20%**]
- Was the student able to apply appropriate cryptography and encryption techniques for different data states and the type of protection available to protect each data state? – [**20%**]

Lab #9 – Supplemental Open-Source/Shareware Encryption Worksheet

Course Name & Number: _____

Student Name: _____

Instructor Name: _____

Lab Due Date: _____

Overview

For this equipment-based lab students are required to download an open-source/shareware encryption application and generate both a public and private key used for encryption and decryption. Students will install the encryption application, generate public and private keys, encrypt and decrypt a file to ensure proper confidentiality is enabled.

Open-Source & Shareware Encryption Applications

Download and evaluate at least 3 open-source/shareware encryption applications from the Internet as provided below:

1. Security & Privacy / Encryption Tools – http://www.download32.com/encryption-tools-33033-category.html

2. TopShareware.com - http://www.topshareware.com/shareware-encryption-program/downloads/1.htm

3. Security & Encryption – http://www.ultrashareware.com/

4. USB Safeguard - 1.2.0 - http://www.download32.com/usb-safeguard-i83038.html

5. Cryptix - 0.85 - MAC OS - http://www.download32.com/cryptix-i83088.html

6. Advanced Encryption Package Professional 5.3.6 – http://www.download32.com/advanced-encryption-package-professional-i60038.html

7. Truecrypt - http://www.truecrypt.org/

8. Choose one of the three software tools evaluated and perform a demonstration in class of its uses

9. Explain what you like and dislike about the open-source/shareware encryption tools you reviewed

Current Version Date: 07/27/2011

Lab #9 – Assessment Worksheet

Apply Encryption to Mitigate Risk Exposure

Course Name & Number: _____

Student Name: _____

Instructor Name: _____

Lab Due Date: _____

Overview

The students will review the encryption mechanisms involved with implementing a PKI and the different methods of encryption needed to provide different functions within a PKI. They will also use an open-source or shareware encryption/decryption application to carry out digital signatures and secure communications. Hashing, symmetric encryption and asymmetric encryption are all covered during this hands-on demonstration.

Lab Assessment Questions & Answers

1. If you are using corporate e-mail for external communications that contain confidential information, what other security countermeasure can you employ to maximize the confidentiality of e-mail transmissions through the Internet?

2. Explain the role of a Certificate Authority and its obligations in authenticating the person or organization and issuing digital certificates.

3. What would a successful Subversion Attack of a CA result in?

4. What encryption mechanisms are built into Microsoft Windows XP Professional?

5. Could you add user's access to view your EFS encrypted files and folders? If so, how?

6. What would be needed by any Law Enforcement agency to decrypt encrypted messages easily?

7. What is SHA1, and what is it used for? Is it used similarly to TripleDES or are they different?

8.   Provide an explanation for the difference between symmetric keys and asymmetric keys in a PKI.

9.   What is a common drawback to Encrypting using enterprise level tools such as PGP?

10. What is the difference between PGP and GPG?

Current Version Date: 07/27/2011

Laboratory #10

Lab #10: Use Reconnaissance, Probing, & Scanning to Identify Servers and Hosts

Learning Objectives and Outcomes

Upon completing this lab, students will be able to complete the following tasks:

- Mitigate risk from unauthorized access to IT systems through proper testing, port scanning, and vulnerability assessment scanning

- Perform an IP discovery using ZenNmap GUI and generate a graphic of all IP hosts on the targeted IP subnetwork

- Identify the operating systems for each of the identified IP hosts on the targeted IP subnetwork from the OS fingerprint results

- Perform a vulnerability assessment scan on a targeted IP subnetwork and identify any critical software vulnerabilities on the targeted IP subnetwork

- Develop an access control and vulnerability remediation plans for mitigating identified risks, threats, and vulnerabilities from the various scans performed

Required Setup and Tools

This lab requires that the instructor and student workstations and VMs be connected to the shared, classroom layer 2 switch and physically disconnected from the classroom/building network and public Internet. This will also allow the Instructor to enable the shared, DHCP server to be used for all the VMs used in this equipment-based lab.

NOTE: The instructor will enable the lab's DHCP server by powering on the "DHCPWindows01" server which will allocate a source IP host address to all workstations and VMs enabled. Only 1 DHCP server should be enabled for IP host address allocation on the same IP subnetwork at a given time.

The following equipment is required for this equipment-based lab:

A) Student classroom workstations (with at least 2GB RAM) capable of supporting the removable hard drive with the VM server farm and up to 2 simultaneously running VMs.

Current Version Date: 07/27/2011

> **NOTE:** Only one VM will be running at full speed on a workstation with only 2GB of RAM. If you power-on 2 VMs at once on a workstation with only 2GB of RAM, there will be performance slowdown. For optimal performance, load 2 or more VMs with at least 4GB of RAM in your workstation.

B) Instructor workstations (with at least 4 Gig RAM) that shall act as the Instructor's demo lab workstation. The instructor will display the Instructor VM or other Server Farm VMs on the LCD projector to demo the loading and configuring of the VM Server Farm and execute demonstrations of the equipment-based labs using VMware Player.

C) Student workstations will use their own VM Server Farm. VMware Player will be used to run the VMs on both Instructor and Student workstations. It is strongly recommended that the VMs be copied to the local classroom workstation whenever possible to improve performance.

The following summarizes the setup, configuration, and equipment needed to perform Lab #10: "TargetWindows01" is a Windows 2003 Standard Server VM used with VM Server Farm v2. "TargetWindows02" is a newer Windows 2008 Standard Server VM that was released as an upgrade to VM Server Farm v2. "TargetWindows02" VM is now part of the VM Server Farm v3.

Although the "TargetWindows02" 2008 Server is not mandatory to perform this equipment-based lab, it is a more up to date VM to be performing this equipment-based lab.

1. The VM Server Farm (Version 2 or higher) with the following VMs:
a. A Target Windows 2003 Standard Server VM ("TargetWindows01"); or
b. A Target Windows 2008 Standard Server VM ("TargetWindows02")
2. A standard classroom workstation must have the following software applications loaded to perform this lab:
a. VMware Player 3.x
b. Microsoft Office 2007 or higher for Lab Assessment Questions & Answers

Nessus® v4.2.2 Vulnerability Assessment & Scanning Software

Training: Nessus® and Network Scanning Curriculums

If your information security teaching/training organization uses Nessus® in your curriculum to teach students how to scan for network vulnerabilities, the Tenable license allows you to use the HomeFeed subscription for your training purposes as can be found in Tenable's HomeFeed Licensing Agreement.

Current Version Date: 07/27/2011

Program Rights, Requirements and Limitations:

You are permitted to copy/build images and redistribute Tenable's Nessus® and Tenable HomeFeed Plugins to students in and for the classroom setting only. Upon completion of the class, the ability to use the Plugins provided by the HomeFeed is terminated and students must re-register for either a HomeFeed or a ProfessionalFeed according to their intended use, as governed by the Subscription Agreement.

Information security organizations and students are not permitted to use the HomeFeed in a commercial fashion to secure their organization's or third party networks. It is only to be used for demonstration and teaching purposes in structured class environment.

If you qualify for the right to use a Tenable subscription for your teaching/training organization, you are required to review the license agreement in its entirety.

You will have the right and may use the Nessus® logo in your marketing of the class(es). If you choose to use the Nessus® logo, it must always be accompanied by the following: "Nessus® is a Registered Trademark of Tenable Network Security, Inc."

Tenable reserves the right to revoke a free subscription or terminate a subscription at its sole discretion at any time.

Nessus® Overview

Nessus® performs remote scans and audits of Unix, Windows, and network infrastructures. Nessus® can perform a network discovery of devices, operating systems, applications, databases, and services running on those devices.

Any non-compliant hosts running applications such as peer-to-peer, spyware or malware (worms, Trojans, etc.) are detected and identified. Nessus® is capable of scanning all ports on every device and issue remediation strategy suggestions as required.

Nessus® includes the ability to perform in-depth web application audits that identify vulnerabilities in custom built applications. Custom web applications can have their operating system, application, and SQL database audited and hardened against a variety of industry best practices and recommendations.

Current Version Date: 07/27/2011

Recommended Procedures

Equipment-Based Lab #10 – Student Steps

Students should perform the following steps:

1. Using your classroom workstation research the following topics:

   a. Network Vulnerability Plan Development

   b. Network Vulnerability Scanning and Remediating

   c. Network Penetration Testing

   d. OS discovery

   e. Footprinting, Enumerating, etc.…

2. Connect your student-removable hard drive into a classroom workstation

3. Power on your Student VM workstation and login using the following credentials:

   Login ID: "student" (case sensitive)

   Password: "ISS316Security" (case sensitive)

4. Perform a quick review and discussion on the subjects of:

   a. Network Vulnerability Plan Development

   b. Network Vulnerability Scanning and Remediating

   c. Network Penetration Testing

   d. OS discovery

   e. Footprinting, Enumerating, etc…

5. Load ZeNmap GUI from the Instructor VM from you Desktop or (Start -> All Programs -> Nmap -> Select Nmap – Zenmap GUI)

6. Power-on only ONE of the following Target Windows Servers available in the VM server farm: "TargetWindows01" OR "TargetWindows02" (pause the Instructor/Student VM if necessary)

7. Target Windows Server Logons and Computer Information is as follows:

   a. Usernames: "administrator", "instructor", OR "student" (without quotes)

   b. Password: "ISS316Security" (without quotes, case sensitive)

8. Obtain the IP address of the Target Windows Server by typing "ipconfig" at the DOS > prompt

9. Enter the target IP subnet number in the ZeNmap Target IP address field: "172.30.0.0/24"

10. Select "Intense Scan" from the drop-down menu and click the "Scan" button to start

11. The instructor will perform the security scan on the server farm IP subnet (172.30.0.0/24) as well as IP network infrastructure if available. And then display the various reports that ZeNmap GUI generates

Current Version Date: 07/27/2011

12. Save your Intense Scan of the server farm IP subnet and submit this as part of your lab deliverables – Click 'Scan' -> 'Save Scan' and select a destination to save the report

13. Load the Nessus® v4.2.2.2 Server Manager in the Instructor VM

    a. Start- All Programs – Tenable Network Security – Nessus Server Manager

    b. Click 'Manage Users'

    c. Click the '+' button to add users or 'Edit' to designate username passwords

14. Open a browser window and connect to the Nessus® v4.2.2.2 Server Manager via an HTTPS:// connection

15. Connect to the Nessus® v4.2.2.2 Server Manager via an HTTPS:// secured browser connection in the navigation bar as follows: https:// [server IP]:8834/

16. Prior to conducting a vulnerability scan, a policy definition is required, and this is what will be demonstrated. A policy definition consists of configuration parameters for performing the vulnerability scan and includes the following:

    a. Parameters that control technical aspects of the scan such as timeouts, number of hosts, type of port scanner and more

    b. Credentials for local scans (e.g., Windows, SSH), authenticated Oracle Database scans, HTTP, FTP, POP, IMAP or Kerberos based authentication

    c. Granular family or plug-in based scan specifications

    d. Database compliance policy checks, report verbosity, service detection scan settings, UNIX compliance checks and more

17. Once you have connected to a Nessus® server, you can create a custom policy by clicking on the "Policies" option on the bar at the top and then "+ Add" button on the right. The "Add Policy" screen will be displayed

18. Note that there are four configuration tabs: General, Credentials, Plug-ins and Preferences. For most environments, the default settings do not need to be modified, but they provide more granular control over the Nessus® scanner operation

    • General Tab – allows you to name your policy and define the scan related operations

    • Credentials Tab – The Credentials tab allows you to configure the Nessus® scanner to use authentication credentials during scanning. By configuring credentials, it allows Nessus® to perform a wider variety of checks that result in more accurate scan results

    • Plug-Ins Tab - enables the user to choose specific security checks by plug-in family or individual checks

Current Version Date: 07/27/2011

- Preferences Tab - includes means for granular control over scan settings. Selecting an item from the drop-down menu will display further configuration items for the selected category. Note that this is a dynamic list of configuration options that is dependent on the plug-in feed, audit policies and additional functionality that the connected Nessus® scanner has access to.

19. After creating a policy, you can create a new scan by clicking on the "Scans" option on the menu bar at the top and then click on the "+ Add" button on the right

20. Perform an actual vulnerability assessment scan on the targeted IP subnetwork: 172.30.0.0/24 and generate a report of the critical vulnerabilities identified

Deliverables

Upon completion of Lab #10: Use Reconnaissance, Probing, & Scanning to Identify Servers and Hosts, students are required to provide the following deliverables:

1. Lab #10 – Reconnaissance & Probing Scan Report – Submit the results of the ZenGUI Nmap scan in PDF format. Craft an Executive Summary aligning your results to access controls and hardening any identified weaknesses

2. Lab #10 – Vulnerability Assessment Scan Report – Results of the Nessus® vulnerability assessment scan on the targeted IP subnetwork – HTML report

3. Lab #10 – Lab Assessment Questions & Answers

Evaluation Criteria and Rubrics

The following are the evaluation criteria and rubrics for Lab #10 that the students must perform:

- Was the student able to mitigate risk from unauthorized access to IT systems through proper testing, port scanning, and vulnerability assessment scanning? – **[20%]**

- Was the student able to perform an IP discovery using ZenNmap GUI and generate a graphic of all IP hosts on the targeted IP subnetwork? – **[20%]**

- Was the student able to identify the operating systems for each of the identified IP hosts on the targeted IP subnetwork from the OS fingerprint results? – **[20%]**

- Was the student able to perform a vulnerability assessment scan on a targeted IP host and identify any critical software vulnerabilities on the targeted IP subnetwork? – **[20%]**

- Was the student able to develop an access control and vulnerability remediation plans for mitigating identified risks, threats, and vulnerabilities from the various scans performed? – **[20%]**

Current Version Date: 07/27/2011

Lab #10 – Assessment Worksheet

Use Reconnaissance, Probing, & Scanning to Identify Servers and Hosts

Course Name & Number: _____

Student Name: _____

Instructor Name: _____

Lab Due Date: _____

Overview

The students will perform IP discovery, port scanning, services scanning, OS fingerprint scanning, and vulnerability assessment scanning using Nmap and Nessus®. Assessment of the findings and how they related to access controls is the goal of this lab. Identifying risks, threats, and vulnerabilities associated with access controls and how to mitigate them will be presented in this lab. Using the results of the various scans and tests, answer the following lab assessment questions.

Lab Assessment Questions & Answers

1. Describe what ZenMap GUI performs to do passive OS fingerprinting.

2. Nmap can also help define applications that are available on the machines it is scanning. How does it know the application? Is this a reliable method of identifying running services on a target machine?

Current Version Date: 07/27/2011

3. Why would you want to use Nmap before an attack as opposed to after the attack?

4. How does Nessus® differ from Nmap (ZeNmap GUI) and which tool would you use for network IP discovery versus identifying software vulnerabilities?

5. What is the purpose of defining a Policy definition as a first step in performing a Nessus® vulnerability scan?

6. Name the five things you can configure as part of a vulnerability scan in Nessus.®

Current Version Date: 07/27/2011

7. Will Nessus® provide a security practitioner any information regarding remediating vulnerability found while doing the vulnerability scanning?

8. What is the major difference between a penetration test and a vulnerability assessment? In your opinion, should an organization perform both or does one or the other meet all the needs for most?

9. Students are required to save and submit the results of the "Intense Scan" in the targeted IP subnetwork and submit that report along with the IP discovery host graphic. Which tool within ZenGUI Nmap allows you to graph the IP hosts identified using a FISHEYE view?

10. Students are required to save their Nessus® vulnerability assessment scan report in PDF format and submit this as a deliverable to the instructor. Can you test login credentials and weaknesses or strengths to existing access controls with Nessus®?

Current Version Date: 07/27/2011